Cracking the Project Management Toughest Interview Questions

with concise, practical responses.

by Deepa Kalangi,M.S,PMP,CSM

Project Management

CONTENTS

CHAPTER 1: 1
Introduction to Project Management
What is Project Management
Role of a Project Manager
Core project management skills
Organizational culture

CHAPTER 2: 13
Applying for Jobs
Job boards
Resume writing tips

CHAPTER 3: 19
Preparing for the interview
Transitioning into a PM role
Top skills expected during
interview

CHAPTER 4: 27
During the interview
Interview Panel and useful tips
Dress code and etiquette

CHAPTER 5: 33
Introduction
Interview Questions and Answers
The final word

Project Management

Project Management

Thanks to my parents for everything they do and without whom I would not be able to do anything. Thank you, mom for always being my mentor, guide, and philosopher and for the incessant support.

A very special thanks to my husband for supporting me in everything I do and putting up with my long, erratic hours.

Project Management

The intent of this book is to prepare someone for a successful interview and securing a project management job. Additionally, there is a section for aspiring PM's that want to build a career in the project management area. This is one ambiguous piece of this world and some light is thrown in this section for those questions.

This book is not a comprehensive guide for either doing a PMP/CAPM or any such certification.

What you need to know about the author.
The author of the book is PMP and Scrum Certified Program Manager that has been in the IT field for about 17 years. She has driven several cross functional, large, complex projects to completion successfully.
You can know more from her blog www.careerbuggy.com.

What will this book do for you?
This book is written with a pure

and sole intention of helping the project managers crack the interview successfully. Being a PM is one thing and being successful in every interview is another. As any software professional, one can prove their skills only if they can get past the hump of an interview. This book is written for each and everyone that are looking for a strong knowledge base for a common, yet unique set of hard Project Manager interview questions.

What differentiates this book from others in the same subject. This book is written as a guide and guidance to aspiring or experienced Project Managers and is a short, concise, straight forward practical advice with clear examples for each question. With short and clear practical examples, this book is unique in the subject area.

Project Management

Project Management

CHAPTER ONE

Introduction to Project Management

What is Project Management

Let's begin with learning the basic definition of Project Management. For that, we need to first understand what a project is? A definition that you probably already heard several times, but let's remind ourselves again.

A project is a temporary endeavor undertaken to create a unique product, service, or result. This is defined in the PMBOK (Project Management Body Of Knowledge). Because of the temporary nature of a project, there is a definite beginning and end.

Project Management is the application of the skills necessary to successfully complete the project a.k.a meeting the project objectives or requirements within the budget, schedule, resources by continuously monitoring and closing risks and issues. There are other project constraints that are important to note: scope, schedule, and resources. These triple constraints are very important to take care during the entire duration of the project, regardless of the phase, the project is in. The success or failure of the project can be mostly impacted with how well a project manager efficiently manages these triple constraints.

Role of a Project Manager

A person that manages these projects is a Project Manager which is self-explanatory. These projects can be small, medium, large and then simple, complex etc. To further it up, the projects are technological, constructional, educational, health-care. The majority of the definitions or explanations in this book are pertinent to technology or software.

Regardless of the size of the organization or the project, there is a general consensus in some stakeholders that a project manager may not be needed on one particular project. If we look at an example of a project where there was no assigned project manager, all the work (Requirements, Development, Testing, Deployment) has to be completed by the assigned project team (developers, testers etc.); the risk of the project failing in such a case is extremely high because there will be a lot of issues related to time lines, coordination, communication, bridging the gaps between stakeholders or groups of stakeholders. The list goes on and on…. And this is exactly what a project manager is expected to fulfill along with many other core project management duties. There aren't many examples of successful projects without a project manager. So, if you are one and are trying to become one, move on. Get there and feel proud about it. Unless the scope of the work is extremely small and is undertaken by a small group that is co-located, every project needs a project manager.

In some smaller organizations, a business analyst is asked to perform the duties of a project manager. They are basically a Business Analyst/Project Manager. This is primarily because of the nature of the work of the project. Typically, in such cases, the project is very small and deals with a small group of people. Either the budget is small or the duration of the project is small or both of those are small. Either case, such a person will lay out the scope/requirements and also work on the budget and schedule.

In certain other cases, there is a PMO (Project Management Organization) for which a project manager works. And in some others, there is no existence of a PMO, but a formalized project management methodology is followed and a formal project manager is assigned. Whichever may be the case, a Project Manager is required to perform all core project management duties which I am going to explain in the next section of this book. Remember, the goal of this book is to give the best for doing a project management interview and not to explain project management itself.

Core project management skills

In this section, an attempt is made to outline the core project management skills, in a more pragmatic way and not necessarily aligning with the PMI-PMBOK. PMBOK is a gospel for Project Managers and it has to be; because that is one place where a PM can find every process, tool and also a rule that might be pertinent to the project management arena.

The core meaning; the essence of what a PM ought to perform for a successful project are called the core project management skills and also, the skills that are necessary for any type of organization and any type of project. And also the skills necessary to flair in any interview :-)

Please note that there are several other duties that a project manager performs beside the one explained below. This is just to highlight the core skills and I strongly suggest for you to go over PMBOK for a comprehensive understanding of project management activities.

1. Stakeholder management.

2. Scope, Cost and Schedule management.

3. Issue and Risk Management.

4. Interpersonal skills.

Let's look at each one a little closer.

1. **Stakeholder management:** This comes at the very beginning of any project during the initiation phase. A very clear and clean RACI (Responsible, Accountable, Consult, Inform) comes a long way for the project manager, especially in large projects with diverse teams. This gives the

stakeholders a.k.a project team members, a considerable accountability in the activities that are assigned to them as early as initiation phase.

2. **Scope, Cost and Schedule management:**

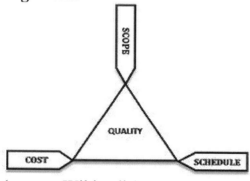

(source: Wikipedia)

Looking at that simple diagram, it is clear that if one of the ends of the triangle changes, the others change too including the one in the center that is Quality. It is very important for a project manager to balance these triple constraints all along the project life cycle right from initiation through closing. The tighter the management of these three things (Scope, Cost, Schedule), the smoother the project runs and the Quality of the project improves and comes as a by-product if you are focusing on the triple constraints.

3. **Risk and Issue Management:** The project manager is constantly on the lookout along with his team to identify new risks, close/mitigate existing risks and also make sure the risks are addressed before they turn into issues.

Risk: A risk is a potential threat to the project objectives. It is potential, so the project manager continuously strives to either mitigate, transfer or avoid risks as much possible to ensure the project is on track in terms of scope, budget, and schedule.

Issue: A risk becomes an Issue when it is not potential anymore and it occurs now than in the future. A project manager assesses the Issue priority with the team and determines the best possible course of action to minimize the impact.

4. **Interpersonal Skills:** There are several interpersonal skills PMBOK lists that a project manager is expected to possess. In this brief section and under core skills, we are just focusing on the top three that are mostly used and useful for a project manager to acquire, hone and use in his/her work.

Negotiation: This is the most used skill for a project manager and it almost always works when used with care. There are disagreements between parties when a risk/issue is brought to the table with regards to schedule or scope or any project management activity. The project manager uses his best knowledge and skills to negotiate with both parties and settle down in the middle ground so it is a win-win for both parties.

Communication: This skill is very essential to the project manager. A project manager should be able to communicate clear agenda prior to the meeting both verbally and in writing along with the meeting minutes after the meeting. Clear, precise communication is the key skill for a successful project manager. It makes him efficient and effective and rewards him with the respect he/she deserves for being a project manager.

Decision Making: Decision making sounds pretty hard as you just look at it from the surface. It is because of the nature and the complexity of the projects or the programs the project manager is put in. However, with collaboration and a clear vision toward the objectives of the project, the project manager can gain the skills required to make key decisions for the project. Not always the project manager escalates to the senior management for decisions, there are situations where the project manager holds tight for key decisions and this skill will lead the project manager to a successful project.

Organizational culture

This topic deserves rightly a very special section on its own because of the challenges it poses even for a seasoned, well-groomed project manager. Organizational culture is very different and incomparable from one to the other. And hence the adaptability of the project manager to the continuous demands of both the project, project team and the culture as a whole is very important.

To understand the subject in a little deeper fashion, we need to understand the types of the organizations and the expectations of a project manager in such a type of organization. Note that this is not a rigid or firm set of expectations, in general, they remain applicable. PMBOK explains this topic in detail, however, in this book we will touch upon and try to remind ourselves the basics of the types of organizations. Three broad classifications are outlined in the PMBOK.

1. **Functional**: These types of organizations almost do not exist these days. There is no authority to the project manager

in this type of organization and the entire authority lies in the hands of the functional manager. So, not much to discuss here.

2. **Matrix Organization**: These are the most common (especially the strong matrix) types of organizations that a project manager most likely is given a project assignment. There are three sub-types to the matrix organization: Weak, balanced and Strong. The Strong matrix organization is the most common type one encounters especially with consulting or contract positions. Weak Matrix is pretty much like a Functional type of organization and with balanced style, the authority is shared between the functional manager and the project manager.

But in the strong matrix organization, the authority lies with the project manager. The resource availability becomes high to the project manager. This is where the project manager makes and expected to make certain key decisions and becomes an integral part of the success or failure of a project. *During interviews, assuming that the interviewer is asking questions in a strong matrix organization type helps the project manager respond to questions in a strong, confident fashion.*

3. **Projectized Organization:** In a projectized organization, the full or complete

authority lies within the project manager. There are resources working full-time for the project manager and there will be reporting staff to the project manager. These types of organizations have several floating projects and many concurrent projects running at the same time. There will be no functional managers in such a type of organization.

CHAPTER TWO

Applying for Jobs

Job boards

In this section, let's look at some important steps in getting an interview call for your application. Lately, it had become very vital to be called for an interview. Even if you are a great fit for the role and the position, you can only prove that if you are given an opportunity to show your skills and the cultural fit. Looking at three major things through this process, the first one is how to apply for the jobs. Let's look at some of those standard job sites to apply.

1. **Dice and Monster**: These are the standard job sites that existed from even before Linkedin has come into vogue; like www.dice.com and www.monster.com. These are very popular site and almost all

recruiting agencies and many clients know and will look for the candidate profiles in these sites.

2. **Linkedin**: While for other technical jobs Dice and Monster alone can find a job for you, in the project management area; Linkedin seems to be working the most. Having a good and clear Linkedin profile with your work experience will let you connect with fellow Project Managers (either PMP or non-PMP) and Program Managers/Portfolio Directors. And many client's hiring managers prefer to connect with you via Linkedin before doing an interview. Additionally, join the project manager's groups and be active in the groups. It is a wealth of knowledge to gain and give back to the project management community. It will help you learn, nourish and get motivated and also get some more eyes on your profile that may help you land in your dream job. If you already have a great profile, it is awesome. Keep updating it and keep yourself up-to date. If you don't, go ahead and create one right away and make some good connections.

Also, there is a new Linkedin app called *linkedinjobs* released recently that helps with a robust job search and for Linkedin members.

3. **Twitter/others:** Twitter is not a job site per se, but seems to be a way to connect with like-minded people if used wisely and efficiently. If you are savvy, create one and make some good tweets, again, make sure they are useful to the pertinent community. There are some people that gained some exposure using the Facebook profile to their career. However, Facebook is primarily a social networking site, so a few updates here and there to your career profile and keeping it simple is recommended. There are a couple of other websites that pull data from all job sites and show you the open positions (and you can also create a profile with auto job settings) like, www.indeed.com and www.glassdoor.com. Both these sites provided value to job seekers in one way or the other, because they pull out all the available jobs in that search criteria across the Internet.

Resume writing tips

Resume writing is a daunting task, but the most important task and also the pre-requisite for getting an interview. Keep the following main points in mind while preparing your resume. All of the tips below are very important, especially for project management roles and hope you consider these while building your resume.

1. **Create SHORT version**- Cannot stress enough on this. Make your resume short, crisp and clear. Keep just the key duties and show the projects/duties in a clear fashion. The recommendation is not to exceed 2 or 3 word pages. Two page resume is ideal.

2. **Summary/Key strengths:** List key or core competencies in the top section of your resume. You can use a small grid/table to save space and make it clear for the eyes of the reviewer. Remember, this does not have to be a comprehensive list, but a key/core list of your skills/expertise.

3. **Do not repeat duties:** When you list your experience summary, do not repeat duties. All key project management duties are the same for every project. For example,

a project manager always does create a project plan/work breakdown structure, project charter, budget etc. Make sure you highlight unique skills/ results on that particular project and don't forget to mention your core competencies on the top section of your resume. That way you are covered overall and then specifically you can state your unique skills/results of the project. For example- if you have increased the ROI (Return on Investment), by an "X" percent, please state so. It catches the attention of the hiring manager.

CHAPTER THREE

Preparing for the interview

Transitioning into a PM role from other roles

In this section, we will touch upon what it takes for someone that is moving up or transitioning into a PM role. Either with a PMP certification or not. As a rule of thumb, unless you are transitioning from another role or doing a dual role because your company wants you to and offers such position with some formal training; you should take some project management training (either online or onsite); whether you write the PMP (Project Management Professional) certification or not. In cases where you lack confidence or cannot show the credit hours for PMI pre-requisites for PMP, it is strongly advised to go for CAPM (Certified Associate in Project Management) for a quick space into project management field and also to get sufficient knowledge to get into a job as you are upgrading your skills or career. Visit www.pmi.org for full information on the requirements and application process for both PMP and CAPM.

Below, there are two very broad categories from which one can transition or upgrade to a project manager role. Both the options below give some guidance on how to plan for a better future/career and also will enable you to find the right position even if it is moving out of your current company. These are tips/guidance only. Use your best judgment based on your personal career goals/options and choose the one that may best fit you.

Transitioning/Upgrading to PM role from an analyst role (Business/Quality)

If you are able to move up or get a dual role that will help you improve your project management skills while performing the role of a Quality Analyst or Business Analyst; that is the safest and viable option. If not, do the following for a successful transition.

1. Read about project management career and understand what it takes to become one.
2. Enroll in a project management course: the on-site course is more helpful for someone that is totally new to this career, but online with a live instructor is equally beneficial for people that are very busy.
3. Become a member in PMI.org. Read through the articles and knowledge base.
4. Join a project management Linkedin group and go through the discussion topics.
5. If you are giving a PMP exam, there are a lot of online resources that give you practice tests or questions and information. Review the concepts.
6. If you chose to just apply for jobs without PMP (as a Junior PM), you can continue your job search and continue with your interview process.
7. Note: If you think you are not able to scale up immediately for becoming a PMP, you can be a CAPM certified first and then do your PMP later. This will still help you with a big push ahead than not having any certification.

Transitioning/Upgrading to PM role from a development role (technical side)

You must be reading this section because you have made a decision or partly decided to move to a Project Management area from being a developer (any). For someone that is moving from an analyst, doing a CAPM/PMP would be the best option.

1. For someone that is moving from a technical side can become a technical project manager/release manager by doing ITIL (Information Technology Infrastructure Library)/Six Sigma or combination, if you want to still keep some of your technical expertise intact and still be in the middle management tier.

2. Read about project management career and understand what it takes to become one.

3. Enroll in a project management course: the on-site course is more helpful for someone that is totally new to this career, but online with a live instructor is equally beneficial for people that are very busy.

4. OR you can take ITIL route and do ITIL (Information Technology

Infrastructure Library) certification
(Foundation comes first).
5. Become a member in PMI.org. Read
through the articles and knowledge
base.
6. Join a project management Linkedin group
and go through the discussion topics.
7. If you are giving a PMP exam, there are a
lot of online resources that give you
practice tests or questions and
information. Review the concepts.
8. If you chose to just apply for jobs without
PMP (as a Junior PM), you can
continue your job search and continue
with your interview process.

Note: For someone transitioning from a
technical side, you can do both, ITIL and
PMP for better opportunities and faster
growth in your career. Again, you can also
do an ITIL, CAPM combination as well,
either of these will put you in a better
position to achieve the project management
career.

Top skills expected from a project manager during interview

The most common mistake that an experienced Project Manager does while preparing for the interview is assuming that all projects are the same and the expectation of a project manager in general during an interview would be the same. But, in reality, it is different. The hiring managers are constantly looking for the following top traits in a project manager that they want to hire.

1. Crisp and clear response with examples: This is by far the most important skill of all. Just not for project management alone, in every technical interview. We all know that examples work very well with all ages and kinds of people. It gives a quick visual in front of the eyes of the hiring manager and would be quick to grasp your skills and experience if you use pertinent examples during the interview. The examples could be newer or even older, it would not matter to the interviewer as long as they are pertinent, clear and convey the response well.

2. Do not divert, stay on the topic: Because of the very nature of the questions in a project management interview, it is very easy to divert from the subject of the question put forward. The processes are very linked and iterative (PMBOK does mention this), so it becomes challenging to respond at the right level and with the right content. But keep in mind, when practicing your material or reviewing the interview questions and answers in the next section, to stay on the topic and be clear in the response.

3. Use numbers wherever possible: NUMBERS-Yes, numbers are the most liked by the senior management. Everything is numbers for them, in terms of metrics, graphs, percentages, dollar amounts, schedule hours, resource counts, applications installed etc. The list goes on and on. So, wherever, whenever possible, use numbers. For example, if the budget of the project was 1million and you stayed within the budget, say so. If there was an overrun or an underrun, also you can say so but with a strong reason why it had turned that way (of course more for the overrun). Some projects are totally top-down, a.k.a worked backward, dates are dictated by the top management and are schedule based. Some schedule based projects are talked in hours, for example, 10,000 hours or 2400 hours etc. The key is to use those numbers wherever applicable based on the question and highlight your role and

how successful the project was that you
handled.

CHAPTER FOUR

During the interview

Interview Panel and useful tips

In this section, you will see what type of interview process and panel, in general, is set up for interviewing for a project manager role. This is basically for the technology or the software folks/field. And the domain could be anything- Retail, Telecommunications, Healthcare etc. Most likely the following is the process and the panel.

Step#1: This first step can be divided into two ways. Once the resume is selected for candidate interview, either there will be a straight phone interview with the Human Resource/Recruiting people or directly from a Project Manager for an initial screening. OR in some cases, there will be a set of challenging questions sent to you by the Human Resources department to be completed within a stipulated amount of time. In the case of questions, there will be a review of the responses before you are invited for a phone interview. In almost 99% of the times, there will be a phone interview prior to the on-site or in-person interview. Note that for some contracting roles, especially with the ones that are non-local, there will probably be just one phone or Skype interview and the hiring manager/client may choose to hire after that first round itself.

Step#2: The second step usually is an on-site interview. During this on-site interview, there will be a panel sitting with you: Project Manager(s) and Program Manager and Manager of Project Managers or Portfolio Director. Typically there are 4-5 other people during the on-site interview and the standard minimum time is 2-3 hours or some people choose to combine steps #2 and #3 and do the whole day, like 10-4 or something like that.

Step#3: This is the final round of any interview process. If both steps #1 and #2 were successful, you will be called for the final round of the interview process. In this final conversation, there will be salary questions and more toward the cultural fit type of questions or conversations. Usually, you have some of the same set of people in step#2 or if the higher management is missing in step#2, they are definitely present during this conversation with the candidate. Usually, during this time, it is definitely a Portfolio Director or the Manager of PM's sitting in the panel.

After those three rounds of interviews, there will be a phone call from the Human Resources department and this is the time to celebrate :-) They come with a verbal offer which time you can negotiate the salary. Usually, a 10-15% range from the offer is acceptable to the client.

Dress code and etiquette

After you complete the phone or Skype interviews, the last round is the face to face. **Impressions do count here.** It is with any interview for any type of role but gets a little particular with project management. For someone that is aspiring to be into the management role, the dressing and etiquette play a big part.

Follow these simple, easy rules when doing an on-site interview with the client. **Wear business professional attire.**

There is no second thought about the dress code. You must present yourself in the best professional way possible. For women, please note not to put too much perfume or too much makeup. Make it simple, clean looking in terms of hairstyle, dressing, and makeup.

Smile always and look straight into their eyes.

You must have heard this many times by now, but never an understatement. Smile always, even if you don't know an answer to their question. You say, you don't know, but with a smile and looking straight into their eyes. You are not expected to make miracles by saying all responses, you are expected to make impressions, the positive impressions. So, remember to smile.

Be Confident.

Always sound strong, firm, yet polite. Which means showing confidence in both the look and the tone. Using the right tone and context for any response is the key to the success during the interview. Even when you don't know a response to a question, say 'I don't know,' boldly.

Never talk over or start too soon

Don't try to respond too quickly before the question is finished. Even if you are enthusiastic to jump in and give your share of the knowledge. Let the hiring manager complete the question and then you start responding. Some people have the tendency to repeat part of the question in response to some questions but pay attention to the repetition. Avoid all repetitions, even though it is totally related. It gives a jarring effect on the impression of the person trying to listen to you keenly.

Mute your cell phone.

This seems to be pretty obvious. Yes, that is true. But with the way we are relying on phones these days, there is a high possibility to forget to switch off or putting the cell phone on vibrate or silent mode. Silent mode is even better than vibrate because there is absolutely no distraction.

CHAPTER FIVE

Interview Questions and Answers

Introduction

In this section, you will get the top 70 interview questions asked during interviews with answers, examples, and reference to PMBOK sections as applicable. These are the most commonly asked questions and also a unique set of complex questions. A sincere effort is made to give as much information as possible to the reader so they can understand, correlate, comprehend the response as much possible, but never a replacement to an actual response. This definitely serves as a strong reference for any interview level and aids the reader understand, review, comprehend to give a clear, concise response to an interview question. Make notes against each question by giving your own work examples to enhance/gear the response to your specific work examples. The examples given in the response are just for reference purposes and not a replacement to your experience.

Not all questions have both guidance and reference. Use your best judgment to make notes, refer to your experience, resume, PMBOK pertinent sections to respond to these questions during the interview.

I hope you have success for your interviews in the future as a Project Manager.

Questions and Answers

1. So, tell me about yourself...

Rationale: This is a very standard question. This applies to every role while looking for a job. The response should always be concise, straight and yet telling everything about yourself. Start with what your beginning title was (example: business analyst, programmer, marketing/sales etc.), complete in one sentence and immediately move to the title of this current role you are interviewing with.

Guidance: Started off the career in so and so, then moved as a PM. Have been working as a project manager for X number of years now, managing mid-large scale projects. My strength is in applying best practices in project management in delivering successful projects and communicate effectively and efficiently with stakeholders and project team.

2. Why did you leave your last job? What have you been doing since?

Rationale: There would be a reason that you left the job in the middle, state that reason. If your reason was related to a job, for instance, there was no work life balance or your boss felt incompetent, you can rephrase and say, I was looking for a more challenging style of work, that will enable my skills to grow.

Guidance: It was a contract job and it ended its term.

3. What are you looking for in your next job?

Rationale: Imagine or think of how you want to be in the next few years in terms of growth and what opportunities you want to explore. If there is a particular area - either technically or otherwise, write it down and use it to respond for this or similar questions.

Guidance: A simple response could be: Growth and learning as a Project Manager.

4. What types of projects have you run? What was the typical size, in terms of resources and budget?

Rationale: For this response, make sure you tell about your biggest team and project that you handled in your experience. Name the client even if it was relatively older experience and give a clear response. Write down the schedule, cost, resources for each project on your resume prior to the interview. Certain times, we tend to forget to talk in the form of numbers, especially for older projects. It is always better to keep a copy of your resume and write down the basics of the project.

Guidance: 30-40 team size, strong matrix organization. Handled multiple projects, small to large and give a budget range that you managed, for example from 1million to 4million.

5. How do you handle starting up and staffing a new project?

Rationale: A new project always comes with its own set of challenges. According to PMBOK, and experience as a PM, even though you are not assigned PM during project charter phase, any standard project has to go through initiation phase and in which we certainly need to do stakeholder management/RACI matrix (R-Responsible, A- Accountable, C- Consult, I- Inform). Based on the charter, you get the business case, high level budget/size of the project. You will then analyze the functional areas by talking to the business in a more structured manner out of which you get the idea of the staff including their skills.

Guidance: A couple of examples here: (Note that these are just a guidance and not a replacement for the response based on your work experience)

1. Based on the scope of Project management plan and the business case, I would start looking for expertise in that area by talking to other managers and key stakeholders. I would start this early in initiation phase and work my way up to the planning phase by when I would have all the requirements fleshed out. That way I am staffing the right people and at the right time.

2. That is something I would love to do and be able to do successfully in the past. I have built teams initially based on the business case, project size and the need. One example is from Project XYZ and Client ABC- I have made a preliminary analysis of budget and resources based on the business case and analyzed options for the build, buy, outsource. The outcome was to build a new xxx project in house and then I estimated the development/testing efforts. To reduce costs, during initiation I staffed only 2 people that had excellent skills in the area and would bring domain expertise and then increased the staff based on the need of the project to meet project objectives. My goal as a PM has always been reducing costs while maximizing output and make the project successful.

6. Have you ever recovered a troubled project?

Rationale: A Troubled project is not something new. Most projects suffer either from schedule overrun or cost overrun or resource constraints. If the PM is brought in later than initiation or planning phase on a troubled project, the PM has to be extremely efficient to bring it back on track. Obviously, the client would be looking for such an expertise. Keep the following steps in mind to recover from a troubled project.

1. Review the current work break down structure or the project plan as a first step.
2. Analyze the gaps, you would look at cost and schedule variances. And most definitely they will be in negative numbers.
3. Revise the work break down structure, tighten it up. Engage resources as quickly possible, do close monitoring.
4. Think of schedule compression techniques *(PMBOK Guide fifth ed- Page 180, Section 6.6.2.7)*: if there is budget left and schedule is an issue, add skilled resources immediately, if both cost and schedule are over; work on achieving the critical path tasks first and foremost. Bring the variances down.
When responding to this type of a question, it is always a good idea to name the client, and

use numbers. Again, you can use by saying, when I took the project, I had seen a -15% variance in cost or a -20% variance in schedule etc.

7. What are you most proud of as a project manager? What was your best project?

Rationale: First half of the question: This is tricky to respond. But during your experience as a PM, you would have noticed certain strong interests and strengths in you. You could use one of those to portray both your interest and pride for the first half of the question.

Guidance: My success rate as a PM had been very high. It gives me immense pride when bringing a project to closure successfully surpassing all the roadblocks, taking challenges all along the way. It makes me feel proud. Or if you were once a programmer/tech person, you could also say that it had helped your thinking logically and hence had been instrumental in putting the project back on track whenever it was deviating.

*Rationale: **For the second half of the question**-* The best project, in essence, should be your worst project. The one that was most challenging, like the troubled project.

Guidance: You would use that as an example to show that it was your best project because you were able to bring the project back on track and in the end, it was successful. Name the project and the client so emphasize on why it was your best project.

8. How do you estimate cost on your project?

Rationale: Below are the commonly used steps for estimating cost of a project. PMBOK outlines certain cost estimation techniques and formulas, however, many companies follow these simple steps to estimate cost of their project.

1. Obtain LOE (Length of effort) for the summary tasks on the project plan. You get the number of hours needed for the task.
2. Multiply by the resource cost. Budgeting is typically separate for full time employees and contractors. The overtime hours are dropped off for Full time employees, so we track the costs separately for fulltime and contractor.
3. Add costs related to software licensing, hardware procurement, travel costs.
4. Sum it up to project cost by phase.

Reference: For more reading and reference, use ***pmbok fifth edition page 224.*** you can look at calculating the cv (cost variance) and sv (schedule variance). these two are commonly used techniques in companies for looking at cost and schedule variances.

9. Tell us how you measure progress and keep your projects on track.

Rationale: Measuring progress is something a Project Manager does on a regular basis. While many companies do monthly forecasting, weekly status reporting, some companies review their cost variances on a weekly basis. Regardless of the company standards or structure, as a PM, it is one of your daily duties to look at the progress of the project. Typically, a PM follows these steps below to measure the project progress.

1. Calculate variances on schedule and cost (Tools used- Clarity or Excel Spreadsheets).

2. Evaluate the negative variances and analyze steps to bring it back on track.

3. Look at resource contention/constraints if the schedule is running behind. Resource constraints are usually a reason for having your project run behind.

Those above steps will lead us to the next part of the question.

Keeping projects on track- We all know as PM's, close monitoring and controlling is vital to any project success and in all phases of a project. So, in addition to looking at the variances, you look at Risk log, Issue log, Planned and Actual percentage complete. Ensure risks are closed before they become issues, and issues are prioritized and addressed right away. Evaluate the deviations from the baselines, understand the root causes and re-baseline as necessary and make sure stakeholders are bought in.

10. Do you have a methodology for handling project risks and an example of a risk you handled?

This is an important question and topic, for both handling projects and also for the interview.

Rationale: For the first part of the question: Yes, we all as PM's have a methodology for handling project risks. A typical process would be to maintain a risk register, prioritize the risk based on risk rating and focus on closing the high priority risks first. For which it is essential to have a risk owner assigned and without the assignment, the risk falls off the tracker. Ownership is crucial for any risk to be eliminated or closed. If a critical risk is not able to get attention and is impacting the project badly either schedule or budget wise, there is a risk escalation process. Typically, the risk is escalated to senior management during the weekly status calls and hence gets the attention it needs to prevent further delays.

Note: Not always we use the standard Probability*Impact, but we use other methods to give the risk a rating. This could be coming from a consensus of the stakeholders during your meeting from the experts in that area of work. Referred as an expert judgment in PMBOK.

Guidance: Example of a risk- You might be able to get one very easily. Risks exist virtually in every single project. However, some examples are given below.

1. SOW contract not signed on time- Risk to schedule. SOW- statement of work when seeking services from a third-party vendor. This is a typical risk because usually the process of signing contracts is very lengthy and it impacts the project time lines.

2. Resource contention: Almost always in a large complex organization, the project managers run into resources issue. The same resource will be assigned to multiple projects and hence their allocation would be underestimated.

For further reading, refer to **PMBOK**
fifth edition-Pages 344-345 section 11.5.2.1

11. What are your greatest strengths as a project manager?

Rationale: Think of what your best interest and talent had been. Use that to respond to this question. Some examples below.

Guidance:

1. Set, observe and re-evaluate project priorities frequently. Thorough pre-execution planning to eliminate as many variables as possible.

2. Tight monitoring and controlling, running meetings efficiently with clear agenda and keeping conversations focused with the stakeholders.

12. What are your weaknesses and/or areas you are looking to improve?

Rationale: This question again requires some caution to be used. We all have weaknesses of course. No need to really hide it, but as we make efforts to correct the weaknesses, you learn new things along the process. So, you can tell your weakness but immediately tell the hiring manager what efforts you are making to rectify the same.

Below example is a good one because it has both strength and weakness hid in it. One way it is a strength to see you are persistent, try your best and don't settle for less. On the other hand, it might take longer. You just have to learn to make a proper judgment to determine the right level of work on that particular task.

Guidance: Perfectionism. Because of which sometimes, I take more time and lose my work life balance. I am working on it to improve this.

13. Have you managed people directly? How many? What are your management strategies?

Rationale: The response to this question is straight forward. Give the number of people you managed directly if you did so. If not, you can tell the hiring manager as you have not. Most of the PM jobs does not require you to have direct reports, so it would not impact the hiring process unless the job description says so.

Guidance: For example, Yes, I have managed 20 people during my XYZ project.

Management strategies could be: Prepare RACI – eliminates a lot of conflicts as the team member knows his/her duties well. Establish ground rules, do team building activities, communicate well and get team buy in. The team participates in decision making and remains as valuable to the project's success.

14. Tell us about a project issue (i.e. an underperforming team member, or resource conflict) and how you dealt with it?

Rationale: **For the first part of the question- Project Issue-** You can reply with the most difficult issue you may have faced in managing your projects (if they did not specify underperforming team member or resource conflict). This project issue could be a technical issue, an issue with a contract/SOW/Vendor or a timeline or cost issue.

For the underperforming team member- Per PMBOK and also experience proves that talking to the team member always gives best results. Micro-management puts a temporary pressure on the team member and had never proven to have shown any result. But by talking to the team member, helping them come out of a personal issue or anything that may have felt de-motivated always shows good results. So, you can use such examples for the response. Recommending Steven Covey's 7 habits of highly effective people is a good idea to bring some positive energy and motivation.

For the resource conflict-
Confronting/Collaboration/problem solving is the best technique which is also advised by PMBOK as the best technique and it proved to be efficient from many years of experience in project management.

Reference: For further reading- refer to **PMBOK 5th edition- page 282-283(section 9.4.2.3).**

15. Have you managed remote or multi-cultural teams? How did you deal with issues that arose from working with such teams?

Rationale: Being a project manager is an incessant job. The project manager stands as a Shepperd / Communicator and manager that requires the flair to lead any kind of project and in any kind of culture/environment. So, for global teams, the role demands the PM's to learn the culture of the new country to aid in effective and efficient communication that is vital to the success of any project.

So, if you are assigned a project that is global, it is advisable to do some homework on the country and culture so you are able to broker the dialog in the most efficient way with the remote teams.

Generally, issues arise from working such teams would be cultural differences and communication gaps. Some homework related to the culture of the country and personalities of that team will immensely help the PM. So, you would do just that. Daily communication with the team members will bridge those gaps.

16. How do you handle out of scope requests from stakeholders? Can you give us an example of this scenario?

Rationale: Out of scope requests are very typical of any size and type of the project. So, handling those requests needs attention to detail and a process.

As a PM, you don't outrightly reject the scope request, you would take it to the business analyst that is assigned to the project after your initial evaluation for an understanding on the impact of the project if not implemented. The scope needs to be categorized if it is high/critical to go into a particular release for a project. For this, the business analyst and the project manager work together on some document that clearly states the solution, business, alternatives and risks if not implemented. If it is critical for the project in a particular release, then it will be evaluated by the PM for the additional cost and time-line it needs for implementation after which it is submitted to the change control board. The change control board then decides to either approve the request or reject it.

You can state examples related to either internal projects or from a customer. For both kinds of projects, the process stated above needs to be done for out of scope requests.

17. What type of development process, code, and tools have you worked with?

Rationale: This is industry-specific. The tools, processes, and technologies will vary, but this type of "drill-down" question will be asked. List all the tools the development teams have used for your projects prior to the interview. Depending on the domain (Retail, Healthcare etc.), the tools may be similar or common. It is advisable to list down the tools beside each project so you are not thinking during the interview.

18. What are your short-term (1 year) and long term (5 years) goals?

Rationale: Make sure your responses are in line with the need of the role. For PM's, it is mostly moving up the ladder in the same vertical, becoming a Sr. Project Manager, Program Manager, Delivery Lead or Manager of Project Managers. You can choose your response based on what you like to do and where you want to be in one year or five years.

19. What interests you about this job and company?

Rationale: A must do homework for every position you apply is to learn about the company and specifically what the role requires for that position. Look for the topics that interest you most. It could be related to the business they undertake or the type of work that is on the description entices you. So, you can use this to reflect on your interests during the interview.

20. What qualifies you for this job?

Rationale: This is pretty much in sync with the previous question. You can leverage the same homework/analysis on the job description and your skills- experience combination and prove verbally (in a way that is the sense of the question) that you qualify well for the job.

21. How do you deal with a strong personality?

Rationale: As PMBOK suggests and from experience, we learn and understand that discussing directly with the person in question is always the best way to start as a first step. You can then ask other questions if the work is not challenging enough or may not have been given a role that utilizes their skills well. So, try to delegate work in such a way that they can feel the sense of ownership and can keep them motivated. Appreciate the good work.

22. What is the difference between "Fixed Effort" and "Fixed Duration"?

Rationale: This is a straight forward definition.

Fixed effort is more or less fixed price (some may define it differently). Fixed duration means you have to get it in by a certain date. It may take additional resources.

23. What is the definition of a risk versus an issue?

Rationale: This is a straight forward definition.

Risk is a *future* event that may have an impact on triple constraint (Budget, scope, and schedule). An issue, on the other hand, is something that is occurring in the present. If not handled or managed well, the risk will turn into an issue and then becomes a bigger issue. So, pro-actively identifying and managing risks is very important for the project manager so they don't turn into issues.

24. How do you deal with a difficult/non-cooperative client?

Rationale: This is not an infrequent situation when the companies are in disagreement, some sort of a contractual work you are doing for the client. There will be or may have cases that the client may ask for additional work/scope to be added within the same SOW (statement of work that has the cost/schedule agreement) within the same timeline or budget. Being the vendor supplying services for them and also not refuse them strongly or bluntly is something the PM has to exercise caution for. Negotiating in good terms and with positive outlook, sometimes, giving in something and taking up something will lead into a healthy win-win situation. You can put together a document that can be an addendum (this may vary from client to client) talking about the new cost/risks/schedule impacts with the addition of new scope and discuss with the client in the most efficient manner so they are on board with your analysis.

25. Are you a soft or a hard task master when your team members do not complete tasks on time?

Rationale: For this question, you can ask yourself and kind of self-reflect on how you managed your projects. For instance, you are a hard taskmaster (a little more than being soft), explain to the hiring manager when you act like a hard task master and why do you have to do in that situation. Likewise, if you are a soft task master, explain why and in which situations you acted soft. Now, you don't have to be either or change the way you handle it and balance the style. Being assertive, directly engaged and approachable would always work.

For further reading on leadership styles-
refer to PMBOK 5th edition- pages 282-283, section 9.4.2.4 on Interpersonal Skills.

26. What is more important to you as a PM - Project Management Process or Project Delivery?

Rationale: Let us pause here for a minute and think about this question. If you employ and are married to the project management process alone and consider it as important than project delivery- for fast paced, complex, cross functional programs or schedule driven programs or merger and acquisitions; for any of those examples, it would just stay in the phase of managing the project living by the process.

On the contrary, if you care only for project delivery and not the process, you are risking critically for being non-compliant, which would be a disaster because you are totally upsetting the business, who are the reason for the company to exist.

So, it is important to balance both and apply the project management process at the right level. Even PMBOK suggests that not all processes outlined in the guide will be required for all projects and it is the culture, assets and the judgment of the Project Manager to decide which ones to use when.

With that explanation, you would have understood by now that both are equally important and it is the PM's duty to use the right judgment so you are applying the Project Management Process at the right level.

27. What are the challenges you have faced in managing projects?

Rationale: Note down the challenges you have faced in your projects and also analyze how you handled them. But below are some examples of typical challenges. Remember, not a definitive list or a replacement for your challenges but just a guidance.

To *overcome* any challenges, do not politicize or brute force/use any kind of pushing communication mechanism knowing the situation. Being a hard taskmaster in everything will backfire. So, just keep an open mind, open dialog, empathize and work around your team's schedule and needs.

Even though the question was just limited to the challenges faced, the interviewer will expect how you overcame those challenges. So, it is always recommended to respond how you overcame those challenges even though it is not explicitly asked.

Guidance: These are the typical top challenges for a project manager when managing projects.

Work culture/ethics/personality- All of these three things when drilled down deeper will boil down to leadership decisions, diversity, personality issues, resource contention, overwhelming work hours, an imbalance in work and life. One of these or all of these seemed to be the trend in the companies lately. Which also means, these are going to exist and a Project Manager is still expected to bring the project to success.

28. How do you start your day typically as a PM?

Rationale: If you want to answer this question using fewer words, it will be - meetings, follow-ups, project documentation updates. Really, that is what a PM typically does every day, to put in the most simplistic manner.

But to put it in a detailed way, a PM does a lot of organizing of work- according to the phases of SDLC (Software Development Life Cycle)/PMLC (Project Management Life Cycle). Most companies adopt PMBOK project management phases but have their own process, however, the PM needs to organize the work and identify missing things.

After organizing the PM prioritizes. Mostly the PM looks at the priority items at the end of the day for the next morning so, he/she will stay on the top once the work day starts so as to avoid impacting timelines/ cost/ scope.

Follow-ups- based on the priorities, the PM follows up with the stakeholders, either via email, instant messaging or holding meetings on a weekly or as needed basis.

Financials- the PM also looks at the budget numbers to understand what variances the project has in terms of financials. These are not done every day in most cases, but however, close monitoring is required in every area of project management, so running a report that shows the variance every day will help keep the budget right.

29. Suppose your team is working on a set of items currently and the client requests for another few more to be delivered immediately...what would you do?

Rationale: The Project Manager should take the same approach for both the client request or an internal scope request. He/She should analyze the request first. In other words, you take the scope request and come up with the additional cost and schedule if that scope is approved. Then, you look at your resource availability and see if you are able to accommodate the request. If not, you go back to the client and let them know that you are unable to accept the request because of the reasons and ask them if they can help prioritize the most urgent tasks first. Once you obtain that information, you work with your team in order to accomplish that commitment. This way it is a win-win for both you and the client.

30. Suppose you have tested and delivered the functionalities and at the client place it doesn't work...how do you handle this situation?

Rationale: These types of situations do not happen often. The reason is that you have tested before installing at the client's place. However, if it does happen, based on your previous experience with testing (either in terms of hardware/software/small devices/configuration), you will have an understanding on why it may or may not have worked. Unless something prevents the project manager should have the same resource (aka SME- Subject Matter Expert) work at client's place. This way you are covered if something like this happens and the SME is able to fix it within the allotted time. If not, we should reach out to the other SME's in the area and fix it. Worst case, you should revert back or leave at a place where the client business operations are not disrupted (not even a tiny bit) and complete fixing it in parallel.

31. What are some of the deliverables in the most recent position responsible for?

Rationale: The standard SDLC GATE deliverables are the ones that the project manager is responsible for. In a software development project, the project manager manages the delivery of the product of code via the standard SDLC process. You can give a specific example of the project and what type of business requirement you were managing through successful delivery. For example, if it is an Infrastructure project and you are migrating a system from one data center to the other and you managed that project, you have deliverables related to that, in which case you will have Requirements, Design, Migration of the code, Testing of the code, Deploying of the code and managing through Warranty phase.

32. Have you created the project plans on your own?

Rationale: This is a straight forward question. Being a PM, you would always create your own project plans or at least update them if you are brought in to manage a project during execution phase in which case you would have a project plan, to begin with. Nevertheless, you would have created a project plan on your own.

Guidance: Yes. I have always created project plans on my own. It helps me understand the dependencies, milestones, risks and issues at a much deeper level and aid me in managing the project in a pro-active manner.

33. How do you interface with your customers?

Rationale: Interfacing with customers becomes the top priority for any Project Manager in any organization. Typically, and Obviously, the PM should have dealt with the customers in the most amicable manner. Remember such examples from your work experience and prepare your notes in those lines for such a question. An example is given below.

Guidance: Always thinking ahead, looking ahead and ability to say 'no' for requests outside of the contract in the most amiable and critical manner. Effective and efficient communication and periodic updates on the progress of the work and respond to any questions in a timely manner.

34. What kind of project tools did you use to manage projects?

Rationale: The most common project tools used in managing projects is given in the below example. However, you can make a note of what you have used beyond the ones mentioned to respond to this question from the hiring manager.

Guidance: Have used Clarity tool for budgeting, status reporting and MS project for making project plans. Have also used Excel for budgeting in some projects and also used Visio for making some flow diagrams that need to be presented to a client, and MS word for making Project Charter and other project documents.

35. How would you start a project?

Rationale: Think of your PMBOK guide and the phases. The first and foremost phase is the initiation phase and what are the processes in that phase according to the PMBOK? You will see Project Charter, Stakeholder management (developing RACI). So, starting a project with RACI is a good way to start. See below example for reference.

Guidance: Starting a project with developing a RACI (Responsible, Accountable, Consult, Inform) and completing it will help immensely in identifying your stakeholders and their roles and responsibilities for my project. So, RACI was one thing I would hop on, and if a Project Charter was not signed off, I would complete it and develop my high level project schedule with milestone dates for all phases. Once these initiation documents are ready, I will formally kick off my projects with all the stakeholders identified from my RACI.

36. What metrics would you expect to use to determine the on-going success of your project?

Rationale: The standard metrics are given in the below example. Any Project Manager would have already known that these are the basic metrics a PM will be using typically. There are other metrics given in the PMBOK guide under cost management knowledge area, but the below are the most commonly used and needed for any project.

Guidance: I always have my %complete (Earned Value- EV) that tells me the completion of a task status and in turn allows me to determine if we are behind in the schedule based on my Planned Value(PV). Other metrics are used, EAC (Estimate At Completion), ETC (Estimate To Complete). Cost Variance (CV) and Schedule Variance (SV) are used to determine the variance in cost and schedule for the project.

37. You have a team member who is not meeting his commitments, what do you do?

Rationale: PMBOK clearly suggests confrontation techniques, which means direct conversations. Generally, that is the most effective way to address any resource commitment issues. See below example for reference and also note down your examples from your experience.

Example: A direct conversation has always been helpful with the team member. I would have a one on one conversation in the most amiable manner to understand the challenges/difficulties of the person. In most cases, it would either because of their unexpected time-line shifts from other allocations (from other projects) or a personal situation. If it is not related to their performance or skills, it is almost always corrected pretty quickly by addressing the allocations or talking about their personal situations.

38. How many projects did you handle in the past? Deadlines met? On time/ within budget? Obstacles you had to overcome?

Rationale:

How many projects you handled in the past- The response is the actual number of projects you handled (all small/medium/large projects).

Deadlines met? On time/ within budget? For this part of the question, the response should be again, based on your experience what your actual projects looked when you managed them. For the most part, you would meet deadlines and would be on time and within budget. But there could some projects that were chaos and one of the schedule or cost are impacted. In such cases, explain what specifically was impacted, why it was impacted and how it was corrected.

Obstacles you had to overcome? Most common obstacles the project manager faces are related to resource contention, the standard rules of SLA's (Service Level Agreements) when dealing with procuring services from a vendor and the others are related to overestimation or underestimation on the project. But if there are others that you faced in your projects, use those to describe the challenges with examples.

39. Do you understand milestones, interdependencies? Resource allocation?

Rationale: For questions of this kind, just giving a short answer would not suffice. You should give the short answer and also the definition/understanding you possess for that question.

Milestone: Yes, I do understand. A milestone is a task with zero duration that is used to track important phase end or begin activities. *Refer to **PMBOK guide 5th edition, section 6.2.3.3, page 153** for more information on milestone tasks.*

Interdependencies: Yes, these are the ones that can be at task level or project level. For the ones at task level, for example, task B cannot start until task A ends. Finish to Start (FS) relationship or Task A and Task B have to finish at the same time. Finish to Finish (FF) relationship. The others are at a project level are the ones that some critical tasks are undertaken in a different project that are needed for your project to succeed or proceed depending upon the nature of the project.
*Refer to **PMBOK guide 5th edition, section 6.3.2.1, page 155** for further reading on this topic.*

Resource Allocation: Resources are allocated at the task level. And also, resources cannot be over-allocated, if they are, then your project schedule will be at risk. If a resource is allocated part-time (50%) on this project, he should be given the time needed to complete his/her task based on 50% allocation which will take longer than the person allocated full time (100%). If you are making a project plan and resource plan in MS project, it will show overallocation on the Gantt Chart (a red person symbol) *Refer to **PMBOK guide 5th edition, section 9.1.3.1, page 264** for further reading on resource management.*

40. How would you current (or last) boss describe you?

Rationale: The response to this question could use your strengths as what your boss will describe you.

Guidance: For example, if you are a detail oriented person, you could say that. If you are assertive, critical thinker, amiable, and have delivered projects successfully on time, you can say so that your boss would describe you as!!

41. How would your co-workers or subordinates describe you professionally?

Rationale: For questions like this one and question#40, you can use your strengths and just fine tune them as appropriate to the question and you don't have to exercise modesty for such kind of questions. You can again say, amiable, accommodating, understanding, guiding etc. Based on how your personality is and what worked for them in the past.

42. How do you perform under deadline pressure? Give me an example.

Rationale: Deadline pressures are the times; the project manager needs to be the most composed. So, make sure you are talking in those terms and of course, the reality is it adds stress. To keep stress at bay and ensure you are able to guide the team with positive energy and make the project successful, the PM has to exercise stability, critical thinking and optimism. Stability to keep the PM away from stress, critical thinking is to create alternate ways to bring efficiency, save time, and resources. Optimistic thinking enables the PM to transfer the positivity to the performing team to do better.

Guidance: You could use any project that you have held in the past as an example and state the above that you performed.

43. How do you react to criticism?

Rationale: While the immediate reaction seems to be uninviting to take criticism, a person with a positive outlook will always look for ways to learn and improve from even criticism. So, be like that and say so. Take that as an opportunity to learn.

44. How do you handle team members who come to you with their personal problems?

Rationale: If your team member approaches you with a personal problem, that means they trust you. Otherwise, why would they truly share with you? So, you should first understand their problem, empathize and come up with a collective solution to the problem. And then guide them through the process by making changes as necessary while the team member comes out of the problem slowly. Be supportive and motivate them through distraction and talking with them periodically.

45. Tell me how you would react to a situation where there was more than one way to accomplish the same task, and there were very strong feelings by others on each position.

Rationale: First understand that this is typical in work environment. During meetings, the project manager will have to ensure to bring both parties to a neutral state and then they could get into a more meaningful discussion, so there will be a result oriented approach than argument. So, as a project manager, you should persuade, encourage both parties to come to a consensus by weighing the pros and cons of each solution.

46. Of your previous jobs, which one did you enjoy the most? What did you like the most/least? Why?

Rationale: Use a specific example from your previous projects/assignments. And we all have the best and the least projects for us, so the more specific you are, the better it is for the hiring manager to understand your perspective.

Example: An example could be, "I like project ABC because there was a great project management process. There was role delineation which was hard to get in my other projects and that increased efficiency of the team and me as a project manager. The standard RACI enabled me to do proper engagement during initiation and gave a good head-start to the project during kick off."

Also, "I did not like project XYZ because there was no sense of accountability and the project was totally under-estimated and totally off to the reality. It brought Chaos and not Challenges. While challenges are great for me, chaos was something that felt like jarring because I had to resort to methods that I did not believe would work to make the project delivery on time. I changed as much as I can, in terms of ensuring accountability and process at my best."

47. Give me an example of a stressful situation you have been in. How well did you handle it? If you had to do it over again, would you do it differently? How do you deal with stress, pressure, and unreasonable demands?

Rationale: You could use the least project you liked from question#46 as an example for this question as well or choose a different one based on your comfort. Again, the purpose of the question is to see how composed, stable and efficient you are when dealing with stress and such projects. When you use a specific example, you will also understand how differently you will do it.

Guidance: I held a project ABC for my client XYZ which was totally under pressure. There were definitely unreasonable demands and expectations. There was some chaos because of this situation. So, bringing back every situation to the normal state and keeping myself stable was something that helped me execute the project successfully. I would not underestimate such type of work and factor in all dependencies, critical tasks before making such estimations and committing to that schedule.

48. Tell me about a tough decision you had to make?

Rationale: Again, these are all similar questions that the interviewer is trying to see how well you handle under pressure or the complexity of the project/work. You can come up with your own personal tough decisions you had to make during your previous projects.

Guidance: One simple example could be, "I had to separate my personal life from my work life and balance both for projects that demanded long work hours of more than 60 hours a week. I still managed to bring the balance for those tough weeks by putting my best to the work demands."

49. What are the necessary steps to successful project management?

Rationale: You could come up with your own list that you believe that will lead to successful project management. Some steps are outlined here for understanding.

1. Efficient and clear communication.
2. Foster positive attitude among team members and be stable.
3. Close monitoring and controlling of all phases of SDLC and PMLC.
4. Appreciate if work was completed on time per the schedule.

50. How do you plan for a project?

Rationale: Planning for a project goes under the planning phase. During planning phase your project schedule is evolving, your RACI is finalizing and you are tracking your progress by measuring your schedule and cost variances. You are also logging risks and issues and following up closely.

51. What is important to consider when planning a (your type of project)?

Rationale: As a PM, you know the triple constraints that are important for any project. So, it is important to consider all three constraints - scope, schedule and cost when planning a project. Scope creep will lead to variances in schedule and cost and which will be contributing to the failure of the project. So, it is imperative you plan fully for these three constraints while planning a project and making your project plan. Also, early engagement or resources is required so you are not encountering resource contention later on during the project.

52. What are the three constraints on a project?

The triple constraints are scope, schedule, and cost on a project.

53. What are the five process groups of a project?

1. Initiation
2. Planning
3. Executing
4. Monitoring and Controlling
5. Closing

54. What qualifications are required to be an effective project manager?

Rationale: There are some qualifications listed that are generally considered important for a PM to be effective. However, you could come up with your own list of qualifications that you think will make the PM more effective. Whatever list you come up with, make sure you are able to have a deep understanding of the terms/keywords; should there be a follow-up question on the same from the hiring manager.

Guidance: Communication- clear, concise, effective communication is a very important qualification of a good project manager. In addition, the PM needs to be having great people skills, strong leadership skills, strong problem-solving skills and strong project management skills.

55. Name four signs that indicate your project may fail.

Rationale: Below are the signs that are thoughtfully written as being the common pitfalls for a project. As a PM, you may have understood and experienced other signs that you think that replace these or have better significance. You can use them as well as a response to this question.

Guidance:

1) Poorly defined scope/ Poor project Planning - If the scope is not defined well, it is a clear indication that the project will suffer through its course of execution.

2) A change in business needs- If the needs of the business changes, the scope and requirements change and will become a

candidate for pre-initiation or discovery process.

3) Funding- Securing the high-level budget or getting a sponsor to fund the project is important without which the project may fail.

4) Efficient team/Resources- You need to have proper resource engagement right from initiation of the project without which the project will suffer because of over allocation of resources or to compromise on quality by bringing less skilled people so as to rush the project to meet time lines.

56. When you are assigned a project, what steps do you take to complete the project?

Rationale: In order to complete the project, planning is crucial. A strong planning is required- identifying the major milestone tasks and dates, identifying critical path activities and defining the phases according to the company's standard project management and software development life cycles is very important. If a detailed, thorough planning was done during planning phase of the project, the project manager will encounter fewer issues during the execution phase. Poor Planning will lead to failure.

So, a project manager would plan thoroughly, identify major milestone tasks, dates, identify critical paths, log risks and issues and manage them proactively and tightly throughout the project.

57. As you begin your assignment as a project manager, you quickly realize that the corporate sponsor for the project no longer supports the project. What will you do?

Rationale: Usually such a situation arises when the business case was not strong enough or there was no funding available to support the project. So, the project manager needs to research for alternate options. For example, if the funding was an issue, then the PM can sit with the business and identify alternate solutions by de-scoping certain requirements and still achieve the goal so the budget is less and approved. If the business case needs to be changed the PM should discuss the same with the business SME and also his/her manager.

58. Your three-month project is about to exceed the projected budget after the first month. What steps will you take to address the potential cost overrun?

Rationale: Such a situation arises because of one of these reasons. The initial estimate was not made with proper basis, which means the hours, in other words, budget was underestimated. Or it could be a case where the tasks were out of sync with the dates and the resource was spending more time ahead in the phase and it was causing a huge variance. So, the project manager should look at why there was a variance right in the first month and address the potential cost overrun. If the project was underestimated, the PM should develop a new budget with proper baseline/explanation and thorough evaluation of the work by meeting with the team and submit to the management for additional funding for the remaining two months.

59. You are given the assignment of project manager and the team members have already been identified. To increase the effectiveness of your project team, what steps will you take?

Rationale: For this question again, you could come up with your list of factors that will increase the effectiveness of the project. Some are given in the example below.

Guidance: Constant, periodic, clear communication with the team enhances the relationship and makes them effective. So, a PM should develop such relationship with the team. Also, the PM will follow up on specific tasks with the team.

60. What is "project float"?

Direction definition of a Project Float is the time gap between two sequential tasks without impacting the project completion date. In other words, it is the flexibility of the schedule and is measured by the amount of time that a task can be delayed without delaying the project finish date.

For further reading, please refer to **PMBOK 5th edition, section 6.6.2.2, page 176** *on float.*

61. Your project is beginning to exceed budget and ready to fall behind schedule due to almost daily user change orders and increasing conflicts in user requirements. How will you address the user issues?

Rationale: For this question, you already know the reason, that the budget and schedule are getting impacted because of the change requests. A CR (change request) gets entered when something important was missed and it is needed for the project release. And you know based on the question that the cost over-run has just begun to happen. So, in this case, you would call for a meeting with all stakeholders, identify the issues that are preventing the cost and schedule be on track and prioritize them to get them addressed. Assign an issue owner to those issues, follow up, take alternate routes, escalate to senior management before it gets too late and the cost and schedule are severely impacted.

62. Describe what you did in a difficult project environment to get the job done on time and on a budget.

Rationale: You could use an example from your previous work experience. Think of the most difficult project you handled and if it did not go on track, what went wrong with that one. Basically, all you would do in such cases is to stay on the top of everything. Look at your work breakdown structure closely, revisit and review critical path activities, make the tasks more efficient basically running non-critical path activities in parallel to save time etc. Close monitoring and controlling will immensely help which also means a lot of heavy duty work and daily meetings until the project gets back on track. Both schedule compression techniques - Crashing and Fast Tracking can be used as applicable.

*For further reading, refer to **PMBOK 5th edition, section 6.6.2.7, page 181.***

63. What actions are required for successful executive sponsorship of a project?

Rationale: The primary driver of bringing in a successful executive sponsorship is the business objective and goals. Furthermore, the executive committee will be excited to know the numbers in terms of the profits for each fiscal year based on the project goals to achieve the business goal. The Project Manager needs to have seamless communication, ensure accountability and present the goals and milestones of the project in terms of both business benefits and ROI (Return On Investment).

64. Tell me about an accomplishment you are particularly proud of and what it entailed.

Rationale: The response could be anything that you felt proud of earlier in your assignments. However, to give some ideas and hints, you can refer to this example below.

Example: Recently worked on a ABC project in which the entire program has been underestimated and there were many accountability issues. Being a Project Manager, it was quite a challenge to understand the intricacies, such a large team, ensure accountability and keep the project moving on track. I have successfully completed several competing priority projects at the same time within schedule and budget by staying on the top in identifying risks and addressing them as quickly possible. It was quite an accomplishment.

65. What is project charter?

Rationale: This is a straight forward question.

The Project Charter details the project purpose, overview, goals, and high-level deliverables.

The project overview - A project overview contains a description of the business need, purpose, and product or service that is to be provided. **Preliminary roles and responsibilities** - This section describe the duties of the project team. This includes people who should be involved and why and how they might be involved. This might include customers, stakeholders, and the project team.

Identification of the project manager - The project manager identification designates the project manager who has primary project oversight responsibility.

A description of the project manager's

authority - The description of the project manager's authority outlines the level of authority given to the project manager. This would include financial oversight and level of decision making.

Sign-off - This is the approval required from the project's sponsor to give the go-ahead to the project. 72. Which document will you refer to for future decisions? I would use the Contract.

66. What is the output of the scope definition process?

Rationale: This is a straight forward answer. Also, refer to scope management in PMBOK for further knowledge.

Scope definition process aims at bringing out the scope items and out of scope items as well. The scope definition process brings the requirements documents, both business and solution requirements. The documents go through a formal approval process and need to map to the business objective of the project.

67. How will you define scope?

Rationale: There are a series of steps that are taken by various forms of discussions and meetings with the Business and the IT collaboration. Initially, when the project is proposed for funding, there will be high level objectives and scope defined. An initial phase will be set forward, based on the organizational governance that defines the high-level requirements, scope from a business perspective. Later, the Project Charter is evolved after the project goes through the approval process from the Executive Steering Committee.

Later the traditional Project Management Life Cycle is followed starting from the Initiation Phase where the business requirements, solution requirements and a committed scope is defined.

68. What is EVM? How will you use it in managing projects?

Rationale: EVM is defined as the Earned Value Management. It is a management methodology for integrating scope, schedule, and resources and measuring the project's performance.

Typically, the project performance is measured by a combination of methods. For example, the cost/budget performance is measured by looking at the variances in a monthly cycle by measuring the difference between forecast and actual numbers. The schedule performance is also measured by measuring variances between Earned value(EV) and Planned value(PV) and typically it is weekly progress measurement.

For further reading, **refer to PMBOK guide 5th edition, section 7.4.2.1.**

69. What is a project? What is a program?

Rationale: These are definitions of a project and a program.

A project is a temporary endeavor undertaken to create a unique product, service or result. The temporary nature of projects indicates a definite beginning and end. The end is reached when the project's objectives have been achieved or when the project is terminated because its objectives will not or cannot be met, or when the need for the project no longer exists.

A program is a planned sequence and combination of activities designed to achieve specified goals.

70. What are outputs of project closure?

Rationale: Project closure is the last phase in the project life cycle. You would have lessons learned, documentation stored related to the financial, scope, schedule, any approvals acquired throughout the project. You would also store information regarding the SOW (Statement of Work)/Vendor Contracts as part of closing the project. Some organizations would require you to fill in surveys for support/help-desk teams depending on the type of the project you are closing.

The final word

Congratulations!! You have successfully read all the important questions and reviewed the answers. I hope this book helped you all along your project management journey, whether it is a new job or changing jobs.

Now that you have reviewed the examples, references for the questions, set aside some time to make your own notes on how it relates to your work experience so far, be it an IT related work or totally outside of IT. This will surely help lay the foundation to your rationale in responding to the questions put forward during the interview.

If you are wondering none of these questions were related to the procurement management area, you are on the right track. Procurement Management is covered in PMBOK as a chapter and a knowledge area, however, the regular project manager interview does not ask such questions *unless* the Job description specially asks for a procurement or contracts manager. And those job titles are clearly contracts manager or procurement manager. This book is written for typical and commonly asked important project manager questions.

If you like the content of this book, please rate/review and recommend to a friend. If you like to read and learn further on Project Management you can visit my Project Management blog at www.careerbuggy.com. I intend to write regularly on this blog and would like your feedback on what topics you would like to read in Program/Project management area.

I truly wish great success for your future career endeavors!!